Y0-BZJ-542

DEC 2012

An Insider's Guide to
FOOTBALL

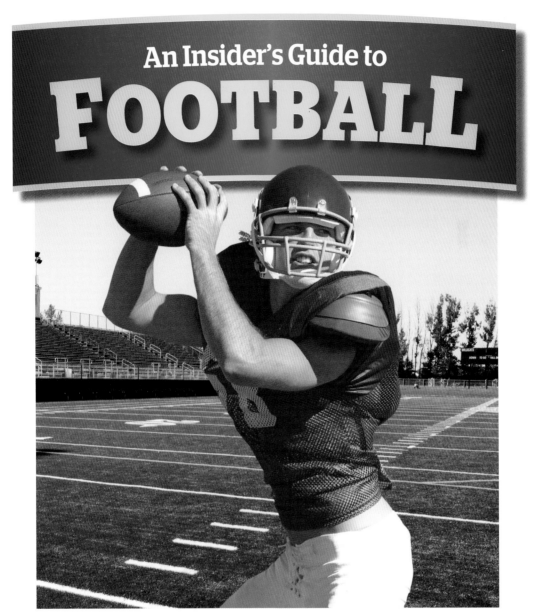

DON VAN PELT AND BRIAN WINGATE

rosen publishing's
rosen
central®

NEW YORK

Published in 2015 by The Rosen Publishing Group, Inc.
29 East 21st Street, New York, NY 10010

Copyright © 2015 by The Rosen Publishing Group, Inc.

First Edition

All rights reserved. No part of this book may be reproduced in any form without permission in writing from the publisher, except by a reviewer.

Library of Congress Cataloging-in-Publication Data

Pelt, Don Van.
An insider's guide to football/by Don Van Pelt and Brian Wingate.
    p. cm.—(Sports tips, techniques, and strategies)
Includes bibliographic references and index.
ISBN 978-1-4777-8585-0 (library binding)—ISBN 978-1-4777-8600-0 (pbk.)—
ISBN 978-1-4777-8601-7 (6-pack)
1. Football—Juvenile literature. 2. Football—Training—Juvenile literature. I.
Pelt, Don Van. II. Title.
GV950.7 P47 2015
796.332—d23

Manufactured in Malaysia

Metric Conversion Chart			
1 inch	2.54 centimeters 25.4 millimeters	1 cup	250 milliliters
1 foot	30.48 centimeters	1 ounce	28 grams
1 yard	.914 meters	1 fluid ounce	30 milliliters
1 square foot	.093 square meters	1 teaspoon	5 milliliters
1 square mile	2.59 square kilometers	1 tablespoon	15 milliliters
1 ton	.907 metric tons	1 quart	.946 liters
1 pound	454 grams	355 degrees F	180 degrees C
1 mile	1.609 kilometers		

Contents

CHAPTER 1

The Accidental Birth of American Football

William Webb Ellis set in motion the series of fortunate incidents that led to the conception of American football.

American football, much like several other great inventions, was the result of a number of fortunate accidents. Legend says that in 1823, a group of English boys were playing English football on their school grounds. The sport was a lot like soccer in that most players were not allowed to use their hands. The players who could use their hands were not allowed to run more than a few yards while holding the ball.

On this particular day, the bell tower was about to strike five o'clock. According to school rules, the game would end with the last toll of the bell. As the bell began to chime, a young man named William Webb Ellis caught a long pass. After catching the ball, he was supposed to place it on the ground for a free kick. Instead, he held the ball and dashed across the goal line for the winning score. His teammates thought this new twist on the rules made for a more exciting game. Eventually, the idea of running with the ball took root, and the sport of English football began to change. Players who liked this different approach formed a new sport—rugby.

The Early Game in the United States

Rugby-style football grew in popularity and soon crossed the Atlantic Ocean. By the 1840s, young men were playing the sport at colleges throughout the northeastern United States. The first match between two college teams was played on November 6, 1869, between Princeton University and Rutgers University. With more than two hundred spectators watching the action, it was clear that the sport had the potential to attract fans. Teams did not always play by the same rules, however, so it was sometimes difficult to arrange matches. For this first game, the captains from each team agreed to follow the official rules of the London Football Association, which were familiar to most players.

The Rugby School in London *(above)* is where rugby was played for the first time.

This first intercollegiate football game still looked more like soccer than the football we know today. The field was large but crowded, with twenty-five men playing at a time on each side. The idea was to advance a round, soccer-type ball over the opponents' goal line. As a player moved the ball toward the goal line, his teammates formed a wall in front of him, blocking and barreling through opposing players.

Players moved the ball by kicking or batting it with their hands, feet, heads, and sides; they were not allowed to throw it. Players were allowed to catch the ball, but they could not run with it. When a player's progress was stopped, he was required to place the ball on the ground and kick it away. As the sport grew more popular, teams kept experimenting with the rules, trying to strike just the right balance.

The Beginnings of Football

A rugby team from Canada brought a pleasant twist to the game in 1874. Players from McGill University in Montreal challenged the football team from Harvard University in Boston to several games. The Canadian players used an egg-shaped ball that bounced unpredictably. They awarded a team a "touch-down" when the ball carrier crossed the opponent's goal line. In addition, the Canadian rugby players could kick "field goals" with precision. The Harvard players loved these differences, and they quickly imported them into the American game.

A Canadian postcard, dated June 1908, shows a football game in progress.

A couple of years later, in 1876, two thousand fans paid to watch Yale University and Harvard play this new brand of football. The next year marked the birth of the American style of football, with the formation of the Intercollegiate Football Association.

Walter Camp (*above*) played a major role in the creation of American football as we know it today. He was active in the sport for more than fifty years.

Looking Ahead

Walter Camp, a young spectator at the game between Yale and Harvard in 1876, instantly fell in love with football. Camp attended Yale himself and was the captain of the football team from 1878 to 1881. During his career, he came up with many rule changes that he thought would improve the game for players and spectators alike. In 1880, the Intercollegiate Football Association started to use some of Camp's ideas. For his many contributions to the game, Walter Camp is now known as the father of college football.

Camp thought that fifty people on the field at one time created too much chaos, so he suggested eleven players per team. Then the field size could be reduced, making the game easier to watch from the sidelines. Camp's most revolutionary idea was creating the line of scrimmage. Before this was invented, each play started with the ball thrown by an official into the middle of a large group. All the players pushed and jostled and tried to kick the ball out to a teammate. This player could then try to break free and score. It was an exciting style of play, but the drawback was that each game was ninety minutes of crazed running, tackling, and fighting for the ball. Camp thought that if a player was tackled, or downed, his team should get more chances to advance the ball. With a line of scrimmage as a starting point, a team would get a certain number of "downs" to advance the ball at least five yards. Teams could run more set plays and use special strategies thanks to the line of scrimmage.

Making the Pass

The game that Walter Camp played was very different from the game we play today. Football started mostly as a running game, and the sport's first stars were runners and blockers. In fact, prior to 1906, forward passes were against the rules.

Most players didn't want to throw the ball anyway. Early footballs were large and rounded on the ends, like a watermelon. In addition, they leaked air constantly. It was much safer to run with the ball rather than throw a floppy, deflating melon. The forward pass became popular, though, because it opened up the field for more exciting play.

Jack McDonough makes a forward pass in a game in 1921. This was around the time when forward passes started gaining popularity.

In 1912, college football reduced the size of the ball to make it easier to throw. Manufacturing also improved, and by 1924, Wilson Sporting Goods Co. had developed a double-lined ball that reduced air leakage. Soon, quarterbacks were throwing long passes with precision, and burly running backs had to share the spotlight with the more graceful quarterbacks. Today the quarterback can be easily recognized on the field.

Pro Football

As the crowds increased, it soon became clear that football had the potential to become a profitable business. Athletic clubs across Pennsylvania began fielding their own teams. The clubs' communities paid to watch the games and support the teams. Then, in 1892, the Allegheny (Pennsylvania) Athletic Association paid a $500 "performance bonus" to Pudge Heffelfinger, making him the first professional American football player.

Before long, professional teams sprouted up all over the Northeast. In 1920, the American Professional Football Association (APFA) was formed. Typically, team owners were businesspeople who saw their teams as good advertising opportunities. Every team lost money the first year, but the league managed to survive and grow. In 1922, the APFA changed its name to the National Football League (NFL). Teams continued to attract more and more spectators, and according to a recent ESPN poll, the NFL is now the most popular sports league in the United States. The championship of the NFL—the Super Bowl—has become a worldwide event. Millions of people around the globe watch two teams compete for the Super Bowl title every year.

The NFL is not the only show in town. Thousands of fans cheer their favorite stars on the indoor turf of the Arena Football League, while legions of Canadians enjoy the action of the Canadian Football League (CFL). Of

The Dayton Triangles of the American Professional Football Association pose for a picture in 1920.

course, college football is still a grand tradition. And every summer and fall, you can see children all over North America suiting up in anticipation of a new youth league or high school season.

CHAPTER 2

Player Positions

From a distance, it would be easy to think of a football field as a giant game board and the players as game pieces. A football game tests players' physical skill, strength, speed, and athletic ability. It is also very much a mental game, as teams try to outwit each other in a clash of strategies. Each individual member plays a special role in the bigger scheme of the team game.

It can seem confusing at first to see twenty-two players burst into action all at once. But as you learn the positions and roles for each player on the field, you'll see that the game is not that hard to understand. Watch enough football and you'll probably want to get on the field and give it a try.

Holy Cross (in purple) and Brown are poised and ready for action in advance of the snap.

If you have never played football before and are unsure of which position would suit you best, the descriptions of the player positions in this chapter may help you decide.

Forming the Team

The offense, defense, and special teams form the three main groups of players on a football team. Individual players may play on one, two, or even all three of these units. But only one set of players from each team is on the field at a time.

The Offense

To win a football game, a team has to score points. That's the job of the offense. They move the ball down the field and try to score a touchdown or kick a field goal. The offense has eleven players on the field at a time, all working together to move the ball forward.

Marcus Curry of the Naval Academy carries the football for a touchdown during the Texas Bowl against the University of Missouri.

The Quarterback

The quarterback (QB) is the leader of the offense. This player guides the team down the field, handling the football on every play. Before each play, the offensive players get together in a huddle, and the quarterback calls out which play to run. A good QB is calm under pressure and understands the flow of the game. As a play unfolds, the QB makes a handoff to a running back or throws a pass to a receiver. Quarterbacks are usually good overall athletes. They must be tall enough to look over the players in front of them and strong enough to throw the ball quickly and accurately.

This player stiff-arms a would-be tackler.

11

Tip for Quarterbacks: Throwing a Perfect Spiral

- Place your ring finger just in front of the last lace on the football when you hold it. Leave an empty space, and place your little finger between the next two laces.

- Raise your nonthrowing hand and let it swing out away from your body as you twist at the waist to throw. Keep the elbow up on your throwing arm.

- Squeeze the ball just before you throw it and flick your wrist downward as you let go and follow through.

This is the position you should be in just before releasing the ball.

Tip for Offensive Linemen: Setting Up in a Good Stance

- Keep your feet no farther apart than the width of your shoulders.

- Point your toes straight ahead.

- Once your feet are set, drop into a squatting position and extend your down hand slightly inside your near foot, forming a tripod. Use the hand closest to the ball as your down hand.

- Keep your shoulders square to the line of scrimmage and parallel to the ground. Keep your back flat, with your shoulders elevated slightly.

- Continue to look straight ahead.

Wide Receivers and Offensive Backfield

Most of the running plays in football are handled by the running back and the fullback, who line up behind the quarterback. When the running back gets the ball, the fullback charges ahead of him, blocking players from the other team.

Wide receivers usually line up at the line of scrimmage, out near the sidelines. When the ball is snapped, the wide receivers streak down the field to catch a pass from the quarterback. Receivers run a specific pattern on the field for each play so the QB knows where to throw the ball. On a running play, there is no pass to catch, so the receiver blocks opponents for the runner.

A wide receiver attempts to haul in a pass.

Tip for Wide Receivers: Catch and Run

- Catch the ball with your hands first, and then immediately bring the ball to rest against your body.

- Control the ball before you start running after the catch. If you think too far ahead, you might just end up dropping the pass!

The Offensive Line

The quarterback is protected from the charge of the defense by the players on the offensive line. In the middle of the offensive line is the center, who lines up in front of the quarterback. Before each play begins, a referee places the football on the ground. The center crouches down and places one hand on the ball. The quarterback shouts a series of numbers and words related to the play before calling, "Hike!" The center then snaps the ball back between his legs and jumps up to block the defense.

The center holds the ball, waiting to "hike" it to the quarterback.

On either side of the center are the offensive guards. They "guard" the quarterback by blocking opponents with their arms and bodies. The offensive tackles line up outside the guards. The players on the offensive line are some of the strongest on the field. They must have a combination of strength and quickness to protect the quarterback.

Sometimes a tight end will line up next to a tackle on the end of the offensive line. The tight end can run out into the open field to catch a pass or block players from the other team, depending on the play called.

The Defense

The defense is on the other side of the ball. The job of the defense is to prevent scoring, shut down the other team's offense, and return the ball to their own offense. All good defensive players chase the play to its conclusion. Change to "Defensive players should not let up until they hear the whistle blow.

The Defensive Line

Defensive linemen learn to react to the movement of the center's hand as he snaps the ball to the quarterback to start a play. The nose tackle (or nose guard) lines up directly across from the center. At the snap, the nose tackle rushes forward and tries to push the center back toward the quarterback, collapsing the pocket of protection. If a running back tries to run through the middle, the nose tackle tries to bring him to the ground.

Defensive tackles line up on either side of the nose tackle to stop the inside running game. They may also rush forward to pressure the quarterback. The defensive ends round out the defensive line. They stop the opposing players from running outside and sometimes sack the quarterback or tackle the running back by rushing in from the sides.

The quarterback slips past the defensive line in an attempt to make a touchdown.

Marqise Lee of the USC Trojans avoids the defense and makes a dash for the end zone.

Tip for Defense: Textbook Tackle

While approaching the ball carrier, remain low. Keep your weight forward, your back flat, and your knees bent. Like the tackler shown at the right, you want to have your face mask at the near shoulder of the offensive player upon contact. Initiate the tackle with your shoulders and chest area first, rather than with your arms and hands. Once your shoulders and chest make contact, wrap your arms around the ball carrier. Bring your opponent to the ground by driving through the tackle.

The play continues until the ball carrier's knee hits the ground and the referee blows the whistle. The defensive players will continue to pull and hack at the ball in an effort to force a fumble until they hear the whistle.

Defensive Backfield

The defensive backfield is the second line of defense. These players patrol downfield and tackle any offensive ball carriers who advance beyond the line of scrimmage.

Linebackers stand behind the defensive line. They act as a lookout for the defense, trying to guess what play the offense is going to run. Good linebackers combine speed, size, and power. They sometimes face off against a big, strong offensive lineman, but they may also have to chase down a nimble wide receiver or running back.

Cornerbacks defend against the wide receivers. When the quarterback throws a pass, the cornerback's job is to knock it down or catch it himself. (When a defensive player catches the ball, it is called an interception.)

Safeties lurk in the deep part of the field and try to help out on every play. They rush in to tackle ball carriers who have broken through the defensive front line, and to break up passes.

In the picture above, the defender tries to prevent the running back from diving for the first down.

Special Teams

Several games have been won or lost solely due to the play of special teams. These players take the field when the play involves a kick. On the kicking team, punters excel at kicking the ball high and far down the field. Field goal kickers, or placekickers, attempt to send the football sailing through the goalposts at the end of the field.

Fleet-footed kick returners on the kick-receiving team specialize in catching kickoffs and punts and running them back up the field while avoiding tacklers.

This punter kicks the ball downfield to the opposing team. His teammates will try to prevent the opponent's returner from gaining a lot of yards after fielding the punt.

Mike Smith has been the head coach of the
Atlanta Falcons since 2008.

Coaches

A game that has so many players on the field needs someone who is the boss. This person is the head coach. Every team has a playbook, or collection of plays, for its offense, defense, and special teams. The head coach is usually the one who calls the plays or is at least involved in deciding which play to run. A good head coach is very organized. In addition, coaches must be able to analyze the strategy of their opponents and adjust their own game plan during the course of play.

Youth league teams usually have one head coach and an assistant coach or two. (Professional teams have coaches for each position on the field.) Special assistant coaches, called offensive and defensive coordinators, think of new strategies to win games.

CHAPTER 3

The Game

It is very important for players to make sure that they are wearing proper protective gear before they take the field. A football player getting dressed for a game is like a knight putting on a suit of armor before battle. Several layers of protection are required.

The Equipment

Football equipment is designed to protect your body from the impact of a strong tackle or a hard fall. In the locker room, players place padding over most areas of the body that hit the turf. Shoulder pads, hip pads, tail pads, and knee pads help cushion most falls. Thigh pads protect the legs from bruises. Some youth leagues require rib pads for added protection.

Once your pads are in place, you can pull on your pants and jersey. Your jersey has a number on it and colors that identify your team. For shoes, most leagues require players to wear rubber cleats. Your helmet is lined with protective padding, and a chin strap keeps it snug on your head," insert "But even the best designed helmet can not prevent concussions, which are a kind of brain trauma common to football and that can lead to long-term disability.

The extensive protective gear required for football makes the players look quite bulky.

Beginning the Game

Game action begins with the kickoff. A few members of both teams meet in the center of the field, and an official flips a coin to decide who will receive the ball first. Then the football is set on a one-inch plastic tee, and the players on the kicking team line up across the field. The placekicker kicks the ball high into the air toward a waiting member of the other team. The kickoff returner dodges tackles and tries to run the ball back toward the end zone. Usually, the kick returner is either tackled by the defense or steps out of bounds. The offense then comes onto the field to try to finish the drive.

The Dimensions

Every football field is a big rectangle. In the NFL and the NCAA (which governs American college football), the field is 120 yards long, including the end zones. It is 53 $\frac{1}{3}$ yards wide. The middle of the field is lined with yard markers called hash marks. The lines marking every fifth yard run all the way across the field. The yards in between are marked with a small dash on the sidelines. This way, it is easy for anyone to keep track of where plays start and end.

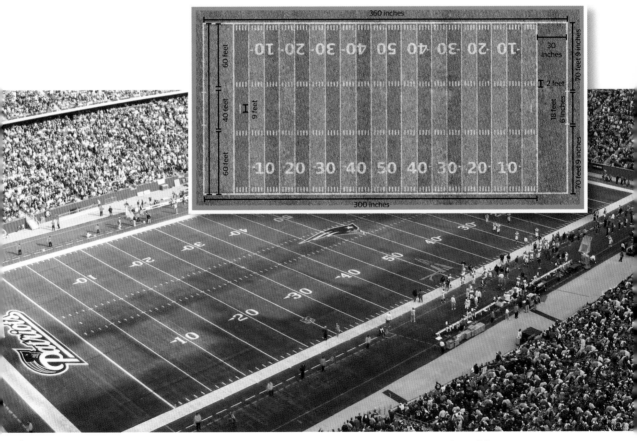

Above is a football field, ready for play, with all the dimensions and markings.

The Offense: Four Downs

Imagine you're the quarterback. Your kick returner caught the kickoff and was forced out of bounds at your own thirty-yard line. You take the field with the rest of your offensive team. You have a set of four chances, or downs, to either score some points or gain ten yards. If you gain ten yards, you get another set of four downs to advance the ball.

On each play, you have three basic choices. You can hand the ball off to another player for a run play, you can throw the ball to a teammate down the field for a pass play, or you can keep the ball and run with it yourself. The goal is always to get those ten yards or score some points.

This quarterback chooses to throw the ball to his teammates rather than run with it himself.

First Down

You call your play in the huddle and then step up to the line of scrimmage. "Twenty-two . . . thirty-seven red . . . hike!" Your first play is a running play to the left side. Your offensive linemen block the defenders on the left side to create an opening for the runner. You give the ball to your running back, but after advancing just two yards, a defensive tackle brings him down.

The down box identifies the down being played (in this case, the first down).

Second Down

Now it's second down, and you require another eight yards to gain another first down. (So it's "second and eight.") You call a pass play. When the ball is snapped, you toss a pass to your tight end, but a defensive lineman reaches up and knocks the ball out of the air. It falls to the ground as an incomplete pass. The play is dead, and the ball will be placed back where it was before the down was played.

This marker marks the second down.

Third Down

It's now third and eight. You call another pass play. At the snap, one of your wide receivers runs forward several yards, and you loft a perfect pass into his arms. But as he catches the ball, a cornerback wraps him up and takes him down after a four-yard gain.

Fourth Down

After three plays, you have moved the ball six yards down the field. It's fourth and four—decision time. You could try a play to gain the ground you need. But if you don't make it, you must go to the sidelines and turn the ball over to the other team's offense. You are too far away to try for a field goal, so it's a good idea to punt the ball away. This way, the other team has a tough time reaching your end zone because they are pinned deep in their own territory.

Punting

The quarterback exits the field and is replaced by a special kicker (the punter) during a punt. The center hikes the ball back about ten yards to the punter, who catches it and kicks it down the field.

Zoltan Mesko, the Michigan Wolverines' punter, punts the ball during a game.

The other team has a player waiting to receive the punt. He wants to catch the ball and race back to your end zone for a touchdown, but your special teams players will try to tackle him. The spot where he goes down or steps out of bounds is where the other team's offense will start with the ball.

Sometimes the player waiting for the punt does not advance, or run forward with, the ball. He may wave his arms in the air as the ball comes down, signaling a "fair catch." This means that no one may touch him and the offense will start at the spot where he catches the ball.

Kevin Faulk, who played for the New England Patriots, catches a punt successfully in a game against the Buffalo Bills.

The punt may also hit the ground if the receiving player chooses to step aside. As the ball bounces, any member of the kicking team may rush in and touch it (known as "downing" the ball). The receiving team will then start its offensive drive from that spot. If the ball touches a player on the receiving team, the ball is live, and either team can recover it.

If the ball is punted out of bounds crossing a sideline, the other team starts its new drive where the ball left the field of play. If the punt goes into the end zone, the other team starts its drive on its own twenty-yard line.

Sometimes the punting team will try to surprise the receiving team by faking a punt. For this trick fourth-down play, the kicking team comes on the field as if it is executing a standard punt play. As usual, the punter lines up ten yards behind the center and catches the long snap. But, instead of kicking the ball downfield, the punter runs with the ball to try to make a first down. Or, instead of running with the ball, the punter may pass it to a teammate running downfield. In spite of being quite risky, the fake punt can change the momentum of the game if it works.

This team celebrates victory after winning a championship trophy.

Strategy During the Game

Football's basic strategy is very simple: score points while preventing your opponents from doing so. But football strategy can be very complex. Even the smallest decision can make a big difference in a tight game.

Temple University's former coach, Steve Addazio, waits to call a time-out in the first half against Penn State in a game at the Lincoln Financial Field in Philadelphia.

Sometimes a coach will try to slow down the pace of a game to keep the ball away from the other team. Running plays take more time off the game clock than do passing plays. So if a runner is gaining good yardage, the offense can grind out first downs and advance toward the goal line while the game clock ticks down. This means the opposing team will not have as much time to score when it gets the ball back.

Some teams try to pass a lot at the beginning of the game to build a lead and then run the ball in the second half to protect the lead. Other teams will pass again and again, simply trying to score as many points as possible as quickly as possible. Successful coaches are also smart game managers who make the most of their available resources.

Gaining Points

There are many ways to score in football. At each end of the field is an area ten yards deep, called the end zone. The goal in football is to advance the ball into your opponent's end zone. This results in a touchdown, worth six points.

After a touchdown, the placekicker can try to kick the ball through the goalposts for one additional point. Or a team may try a two-point conversion instead. They get one chance from several yards out to drive the ball into the end zone again. Most kickers easily make the short kick, so it is the safer option. Teams go for the two-point conversion option only in special circumstances.

Peyton Manning is a quarterback for the Denver Broncos. He holds many records, including the most touchdown passes in the first month of a season.

Sometimes a team's offense nears the end zone but can't score a touchdown. If this happens, the placekicker comes on to try to kick a field goal through the goalposts at the back of the end zone. A field goal counts for three points. In the NFL, the goalposts are 18 feet 6 inches wide; NCAA and youth league posts are 23 feet 4 inches wide.

The only other way to score is on a safety. This play occurs when the defense tackles a ball carrier in his own end zone, or if an offensive player fumbles the ball out of bounds in his own end zone. A safety is worth two points.

Edward Hochuli has been a National Football League
official since the 1990 season.

The Officials

There is a team of officials on the field at every football game. They spread out and make sure that all the rules are being followed. It's not an easy job, as there is a lot of action happening quickly on every play, and there are hundreds of rules that govern the game. NFL and college football teams use seven officials for every game. Other leagues use as few as two or three per game.

The referee is the official with the most authority. He wears a white hat, while the others wear black ones. In addition to the referee, other officials on the field may include the umpire and the head linesman, as well as the line judge, field judge, back judge, and side judge.

When an official spots a violation of the rules, he will throw a yellow flag to mark the location of the foul and may blow his whistle to stop the play. The offending team may then receive a penalty for breaking the rules. In most cases when a penalty occurs, the offending team is assessed a penalty of five, ten, or fifteen yards. Common offensive penalties include holding and illegal procedure, such as a false start. Common defensive penalties include pass interference and offside, which occurs when a defensive player is across the line of scrimmage when the ball is snapped.

Timing

Officials also keep track of the play clock and game time. The play clock is a device used to speed up the pace of play. The center must snap the ball before the play clock expires, or else the team is penalized for delaying the game. In the NFL, the play clock normally counts off forty seconds. In college games, the play clock timer is set for thirty seconds.

Game time is divided into two halves, which are divided into two periods, or quarters. In the NFL and college, teams play four fifteen-minute quarters. High schools use twelve-minute quarters. After each quarter, teams switch which end zone they are defending in order to keep the game fair. One team might be at an advantage if the position of the sun in the sky favors them or if one side of the field is uneven or muddy. Sides are switched to ensure that one team is not favored over the other. After two quarters, the players get a short break (halftime) to drink some fluids and discuss game strategy with their coach.

Football Lingo

Football has its own special vocabulary, or lingo. If you want to understand what the TV game announcers are talking about, it will help to know a few of these colorful terms:

bomb A long forward pass.

clip To block an opponent illegally from behind, usually at leg level.

flea flicker A trick offensive play in which the quarterback hands the ball to a running back, making the defense think it is a running play. The running back, however, tosses the ball back to the quarterback, who throws a long pass.

gridiron A football field.

hang time The amount of time a punt remains in the air.

move the chains To gain ten yards and make a first down; "the chains" is the slang term for the first-down marker.

pigskin A slang term for a football. Footballs were made from inflated pig bladders in the 19th century.

When the offense crosses the opponent's 20-yard line, it has entered the so-called "red zone".

red zone The area between the end zone and the twenty-yard line. A team is threatening to score when it is in the red zone.

rush To move the ball by running.

shotgun An offensive formation, used especially for passing, in which the quarterback receives the snap several yards behind the line of scrimmage.

This center prepares to snap the football in a shotgun formation in a game.

spike The act of slamming the ball to the ground after scoring a touchdown.

squib kick A kickoff in which the ball is kicked low so that it will bounce along the ground, making it difficult to field and return.

zebras Football officials, so called because of their uniforms—black shoes, white pants, black belt, and a black-and-white striped shirt.

Football officials are called "zebras" because of the uniform they wear.

CHAPTER 4

Getting Involved

All through the football season, you can see young children rush out to the field to recreate the excitement of watching their favorite players perform. Many kids dream of playing football themselves and wonder how to get involved. Luckily, there are many ways to play football. Simply getting together with a group of kids from your neighborhood is one way to get started. If you don't want to tackle each other, flag football keeps all the fun without the contact. Stuff a bandana or other piece of cloth in the waistband of your pants. If someone pulls your "flag" out, then you are considered downed. Another variation is two-hand tag football. Instead of tackling, a defender must touch the ball carrier with two hands to stop the play. These games can even be played on blacktop or in the street if you don't have access to a large, grassy field.

Players always line up and shake each other's hands in a show of sportsmanship at the game's conclusion.

How to Join a Team

It's easy to get involved with an organized athletic team if you are eager to play some more. Most local youth league football teams post signs when they are recruiting players for a new season. Check out the bulletin board at your local community center. Signing up usually requires a fee and the cost of your equipment.

There is no single organization that oversees all the youth football played throughout the United States, but some national groups run football teams in towns throughout the country. Pop Warner Football, for example, is a league for more than 170,000 young players in the United States. American Youth Football is a similar organization.

Buying the Equipment

Once you find a team, you'll need some football equipment. Many teams include uniforms when you sign up to play. If you are just starting out, coaches will be able to tell you what you need to buy. If your team doesn't provide everything you need, there are many stores that sell football gear. Some specialty stores carry pads and any other football equipment you'll need. To better

Football is a game that cannot be played without elementary protective gear like helmets and shoulder pads.

protect yourself from injuries, be picky and purchase equipment that fits correctly," insert "Choosing the right helmet is particularly important in order to lower the risk of concussions and the potentially catastrophic long-term disability associated with them. If you can't find a specialty store near you, you can always shop on the Internet. There are some great sporting goods stores that carry a wide range of supplies at reasonable prices.

The Season

All over North America, the youth league football season begins around late August or early September, just as the heat of summer is cooling down. You can expect to practice at least one afternoon per week during the season. Games are usually held outdoors, on Saturdays.

The defense tackles the ball carrier, halting his forward progress short of the goal line.

The regular season typically lasts about three months, with the playoffs carrying the season into a fourth month. Most leagues play games in all types of weather, from blazing sun to rain to freezing temperatures, so be prepared. At the end of the season, the two teams with the most wins usually play against each other in a playoff to determine the champion. There could even be several rounds of playoff games in bigger leagues to determine the champion.

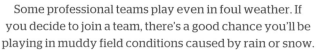

Some professional teams play even in foul weather. If you decide to join a team, there's a good chance you'll be playing in muddy field conditions caused by rain or snow.

Anyone Can Play Football

Football is a sport that girls can play too. For many years, our society worried that football was too rough for girls and tried to keep them from playing. But girls tackled the problem and found a way to play. Today, there are teams for girls at all levels, even the pros. The Women's Professional Football League has seventeen teams across the United States.

Going Ahead

Youth leagues field teams for kids from ages five to fifteen. If you're crazy about football and want to keep playing past that age, check out the activities at your school. Many high schools have their own football teams. Each year, the coaches hold tryouts to choose the members of the team. Some schools have two levels of players. Newer players make up the

There are many youth leagues and school teams that encourage young people to play.

junior varsity squad, and the more accomplished players make up the varsity teams. A lot of high school and varsity teams enjoy friendly competition with other schools in the vicinity.

Colleges and universities sometimes observe the best players on high school football teams. These players are offered scholarships to attend classes and play football for the college.

The ultimate achievement for the football athlete is playing at the professional level. Professional football players are truly the best of the best. Only the finest college players make the jump to the NFL, Canadian Football League (CFL), or the Arena Football League. It takes complete dedication to your sport to be a professional player.

Getting in Shape

There is no question that football is a physical sport. You've probably seen crunching tackles on television. Once you're on the field, you'll find out just how that crunch feels. If you want to enjoy the sport, it is very important to stay

It's important for children and teens to wear the correct protective gear that has been designed to prevent injury.

healthy and take care of your body. Some people worry that football is too violent. Concussions, in particular, are a growing concern, especially for still developing youths. Repeated concussions and returning to play too soon after a concussion can result in eventual long-term disability. The U.S. Consumer Product Safety Commission recently found that players in organized youth football had fewer injuries than other young people playing soccer, skateboarding, or bike riding. Proper equipment and coaching help prevent many injuries. Playing with other young people your own size also helps. Youth organizations like Pop Warner Football follow height and weight charts to place players at the right level.

Injury

Football equipment and rules are designed to prevent injuries. Despite this, players do sometimes get hurt. Some injuries are the result of bad luck, but many can be prevented by being smart and using proper running and tackling techniques.

The most common injuries in football are strains, sprains, and bruises. A strain occurs when a muscle or tendon is twisted, pulled, or torn. Tendons are the cords of tissue that connect muscles to bone. A sprain is similar to a strain, but it is the stretching or tearing of a ligament instead of a tendon. Ligaments are bands of tough tissue that attach bone to bone.

Training

You can reduce the risk of injury greatly by taking care of your body—and not only on game day. Regular daily exercise is a must. Your lungs, bones, and muscles must all be strong. If you are playing football, or plan to play, fuel your body with healthful food and get plenty of exercise throughout the week. Take the time to warm up before a game by stretching your muscles and moving your joints. Also, drink plenty of fluids, especially when playing in hot weather. It's important to take regular breaks while practicing in order to replace the water that you lose while sweating.

You must be serious about your weekly practices if you are part of a football team. By practicing well, you learn the plays and train your body for the full game on the weekend. Players who are serious about the sport often follow specific exercise routines. The best players are not just wrapped in muscle. They are flexible, too, and have the endurance to give their best effort for the entire game. A player in top shape can cross the field in a burst of speed without doubling over to catch his breath. Training and conditioning are as important as any play on the field.

Now that you've learned the football basics, you're ready to start playing the great American game. As you play more, you will find that you can always improve your game. But the most important thing about football is to remember that it is a game, and to have fun - whether you are the star on your high school team or playing flag football in your backyard.

Warming up and exercising before playing is very important.

Glossary

accurate Free from error.

burly Large and sturdy.

chaos Confusion and disorder.

cleat A pointed piece of hard rubber attached to the underside of football shoes to provide traction.

conclusion The last part of something.

contribution The part played by a person or thing in bringing about a result or helping something to advance.

deflate To release air from an object.

endurance The physical ability to continue with a difficult, tiring task.

hash marks Yard-marking lines between the goal lines on a football field; at the beginning of each play, an official places the ball on a hash mark.

line of scrimmage Line parallel to the goal lines where football linemen line up at the start of each play.

penalty A punishment imposed on a team or competitor for breaking a game rule.

placekicker The player who is responsible for the kicking duties of field goals and extra points.

punt A football play in which the ball is dropped from the hands and kicked before it touches the ground.

recruit To enroll or seek to enroll.

revolutionary New and bringing about great change.

spectators People who view a sporting event.

For More Information

Organizations

Arena Football League

640 N. LaSalle Street, Suite #557

Chicago, IL 60654

(312) 465-2200

Web site: http://www.arenafootball.com

National Football League

280 Park Avenue

New York, NY 10017

(212) 450-2000

Web site: http://www.nfl.com

Professional Football Researchers Association

12870 Route 30, #39

North Huntingdon, PA 15642

Web site: http://www.profootballresearch.org

Pro Football Hall of Fame

2121 George Halas Drive NW

Canton, OH 44708

(330) 456-8207

Web site: http://www.profootballhof.com

Girls/Women's Football Resources

Independent Women's Football League

P.O. Box 1844

Round Rock, TX 78680

(512) 215-4238

Web site: http://www.iwflsports.com

Women's Professional Football League

232 Belmont Street

Hurst, TX 76053

(877) 973-5669

Web site: http://www.womensprofootball.com

Youth Football Organizations

American Youth Football & Cheer

(888) 438-2816

Web site: http://www.americanyouthfootball.com

Pop Warner Little Scholars, Inc.

586 Middletown Boulevard, Suite C-100

Langhorne, PA 19047

(215) 752-2691

Web site: http://www.popwarner.com

Web Sites

Due to the changing nature of Internet links, the Rosen Publishing Group, Inc., has developed an online list of Web sites related to the subject of this book. This site is updated regularly. Please use this link to access the list:

http://www.rosenlinks.com/STTS/Foot

For Further Reading

Bacon, John U. *Fourth and Long: The Fight for the Soul of College Football*. New York, NY: Simon & Schuster, 2013.

Benedict, Jeff, and Armen Keteyian. *The System: The Glory and Scandal of Big-Time College Football*. New York, NY: Doubleday, 2013.

Camp, Walter. *American Football (1891)*. New York, NY: Kessinger Publishing, 2008.

Easterbrook, Gregg. *The King of Sports: Football's Impact on America*. New York, NY: Thomas Dunne Books, 2013.

Jackson, Nate. *Slow Getting Up: A Story of NFL Survival from the Bottom of the Pile*. New York, NY: Harper, 2013.

Kirwan, Pat, and David Seigerman. *Take Your Eye Off the Ball: How to Watch Football by Knowing Where to Look*. Chicago, IL: Triumph Books, 2010.

Klein, Gilbert. *Football 101*. New York, NY: Mainframe Press, 2011.

Long, Howie, and John Czarnecki. *Football for Dummies*. Hoboken, NJ: Wiley Publishing Inc., 2011.

Schultz, Brad. *The NFL, Year One: The 1970 Season and the Dawn of Modern Football*. Dulles, VA: Potomac Books Inc., 2013.

Bibliography

American Academy of Orthopaedic Surgeons. "Sprains and Strains." Retrieved January 29, 2006 (http://www.orthoinfo.aaos.org).

Arena Football League. "AFL 101: Rules of Arena Football and the Basics of the Game." Retrieved January 24, 2006 (http://www.areanafootball.com/ViewArticle. dbml?DB_OEM_ID=3500&KEY=ATCLID=99180).

Football.com. "Rules and Information." Retrieved January 23, 2006 (http://www.football.com/rulesabc/play_game.shtml).

Hannon, Kent. "Is Football Safe for Kids?" Retrieved January 10, 2006 (http://www.metroyouthfootball.com/sports_illustrated.htm).

National Institute of Arthritis and Musculoskeletal and Skin Diseases. "Childhood Sports Injuries and Their Prevention: A Guide for Parents with Ideas for Kids." Retrieved February 10, 2006 (http://www.niams.nih.gov).

Oldham, Scott. "Bombs Away." *Popular Mechanics*, October 16, 2001. Retrieved March 13, 2006 (http://www.popularmechanics.com/science/sports/1283226.html?page=1&c=y).

Professional Football Researchers Association. "Dribble, Hack, and Split: The Origins of Soccer and Rugby." Retrieved January 23, 2006 (http://www.footballresearch.com/articles/frpage.cfm?topic=b-to1800).

Stewart, Mark. *Football: A History of the Gridiron Game*. New York, NY: Franklin Watts, 1998.

Index

About the Authors

Don Van Pelt is a sportswriter and football historian and enthusiast who lives in Michigan.

Brian Wingate has been an avid follower of the National Football League for twenty years. He developed a love for the game playing youth football throughout his childhood. An experienced writer in the field of youth sports, Wingate has published books covering soccer, skateboarding, and BMX racing, in addition to football. He lives in Tennessee with his wife and children.

Photo Credits

The photographs in this book are used by permission and through the courtesy of: bikeriderlondon/shutterstock.com; bikeriderlondon/shutterstock.com, 1, 27 © xtock/shutterstock.com, 3, 37; © Cvene64/commons.wikimedia.org, 4; © G-Man/commons.wikimedia.org, 5; © Montreal Import Co./commons.wikimedia.org, 6, 8; © Project Gutenberg/commons.wikimedia.org, 7; © http://www.daytontriangles.com/1920team.htm/commons.wikimedia.org, 9; © Paul Keleher/commons.wikimedia.org, 10; © U.S. Navy photo by Midshipman 4th Class Dominic Montez/commons.wikimedia.org, 11; © Herbert Kratky/shutterstock.com, 11, 14, 24; © ostill/shutterstock.com, 12; © Aspen Photo/shutterstock.com, 13, 17, 33; © Richard Paul Kane/shutterstock.com, 15, 28; © Photo Works/shutterstock.com, 16; © Daniel Padavona/shutterstock.com, 18; © Paul Keleher/commons.wikimedia.org, 19; © Mike_Smith_(American_football_coach)_2013_02.jpg/commons.wikimedia.org, 20; © RTimages/shutterstock.com, 22; © Bernard Gagnon/commons.wikimedia.org, 23; © antpkr/shutterstock.com, 23; © alphaspirit/shutterstock.com, 23; © Tumar/shutterstock.com, 24; © Lowe R. Llaguno/shutterstock.com, 24; © Suzanne Tucker/shutterstock.com, 25; © julia-photo/shutterstock.com, 25; © Erik Drost/commons.wikimedia.org, 26; © flickr user cgilmour/commons.wikimedia.org, 26; © Jack Newton/commons.wikimedia.org, 26; © Jeffrey Beall/commons.wikimedia.org, 29; © Thinh Nguyen/commons.wikimedia.org, 30; © Steve Cukrov/shutterstock.com, 32; © Mike Flippo/shutterstock.com, 33; © Cynthia Farmer/shutterstock.com, 34; © Pixel 4 Images/shutterstock.com, 35; © AngélicaMartínez/commons.wikimedia.org, 36; © Peter Weber/shutterstock.com, 36; © SUSAN LEGGETT/shutterstock.com, 37; © John Panella/shutterstock.com, 38; © PiotrDrabik/commons.wikimedia.org, 40.